FINISHING LINE PRESS

www.finishinglinepress.com

ALL YOU CAN MEASURE

poems by

Lauren Suchenski

Finishing Line Press
Georgetown, Kentucky

ALL YOU CAN MEASURE

ACKNOWLEDGMENTS

"Thump" first appeared in *Barren Magazine*
"No horizon on the map" and *"The slow saving"* first appeared in *Sharkpack*
"What wind" first appeared in *Subprimal*
"Your head" and *"Great feats accomplished mid-air on a flight home to
Philadelphia"* first appeared in *Rose Quartz Magazine*
"All you can measure" first appeared in *Marias at Sampaguita*
"I never wanted to know" first appeared in *Neon Mariposa*
"This tiny forgetting" first appeared in *Passaic/Voluspa*
"I hear your hands" first appeared in *Dime Show Review*
"Beautiful virus" first appeared in *Ellipsis Magazine*
"I follow" first appeared in *Anti-Heroin Chic*
"Submerging" first appeared in *Variant Press*
"Prayer for my son, aged 5" and *"The singular"* first appeared in *Floodlight
Editions*
"The singular" first appeared in *Re-Side*

Publisher: Leah Huete de Maines
Editor: Christen Kincaid
Cover Art: Lauren Suchenski
Author Photo: Ceilidh Madigan
Cover Design: Elizabeth Maines McCleavy

Order online: www.finishinglinepress.com
                also available on amazon.com

Author inquiries and mail orders:
Finishing Line Press
P. O. Box 1626
Georgetown, Kentucky 40324
U. S. A.

Table of Contents

To my son

New meaningfuls

new meaningfuls will come. worry not,
they will come
the cardboard box in the garage
will not take it all—
new meaningfuls will come

angling high and wish-washed dry
the world will give you hands again—
offer you a petal—say cherish this one too

new river dreams will come—
new sandwiched toes between the mud
new hearts red-rich and filled with stories-old
will come;
will be made new again

new meaningfuls will come—
the past will not walk away
with everything—
you have more years to grasp; you have more years to grasp,

gather, gain, grimace and sing

When I was

When I was 19
I could talk to the sunset.
the majestic poles of the sky would
splinter their spines
towards me—wrap their tongues
around my brain
and sing
silent heaving lullabies

when i was 19 the sunset talked back
it squirreled answers away from me
and i ate them
like cherry dewdrops falling
from that opal sun

i rumbled rivers through my bones
i carried landscapes in my eyes
i doused myself in twilight and
i counted stars by name

i do not know
what became
of the silver moon or night
but i remember
that all my smallest wisdoms
came not from steel
but light

Summer math at 6-years-old

Trampoline-river and you; you sprout rock
egged-eyes looking for any prize at all:
the swell of hydrangea, the smell of the air
mid-august, mid-pandemic—mid-plan-less universe
wheeling out endless platters of joy
across the sprinkled branches of summer light;

Creator, you, sound and fury, salt and wind
careening through your lungs—the
softest screams—announcing your presence
upon the roots and leaves;
announcing your self—bounding towards
the discovery of a bug walking across the deck
sliding its way towards the
endless chasm of grass before it;
about to dip into an eternity of soil

You are its lone locator—the explorer
formerly known as you; discoverer of great
things: bugs and beads,
shells and seeds—
capture captain: you have collected
the rarest assortment of twigs and nutshells
and pinecones

the museum we amass
Glitters and shines in the morning dew
and in the afternoon haze;
Half a walnut, a plastic lego missing a leg, 4 leaves, a handful
of pine needles and 18 bark bits
sprinkled across the table—a fossil of summer
endlessly alive

the edges of the leaves curl in,
the stones play against one another in conversation
and the collection never ends—the glory of
today's treasure never tops another's—

It just wonders and wonders on top of one another;
nothing canceling anything else out
Addition of the never-ending sort
just like you, just like you;
grows and grows:
Addition of the never-ending sort

What wind

What wind fails
to admire
the courage of
roots
digging

What blasphemy is
budding on this
tree/
fire curled, rain-washed and pearlescent
The scent of hungered Marches
sinking into branch-flesh

Who is the rain, who is the rain

What spindled limbs chatter
below my feet / fungal-networked
and social climbing
root dominions—
coerced, coerced;
connected—don't you see? The roots are all
conspiring

The branches are all thirst and desiring/

The trunk—
rapturous

Circumstantial words

Circumstantial words, or
coal in reverse—carbonizing back to plantlife—
keep it in the ground, it will form a circle.
A circumstance of stances not taken yet;
dances still flirting in disrepose /
I said—to me, you are the alwaysman,
You said I cannot remember the shape of your hand, or
why you think mine should fit in yours

Heavy metals, though, they need supernovae to form /
We can manage it—
large hadron collider and such,
but the time
it will take
to match gravity
pales
in comparison
to your memory /
My circumstance;
atomic structure;
quizzical destiny looking itself up in the dictionary;
situational comedy;
resonance;
and circumstance
—
like two timelines clinking champagne glasses—
a salute to our cellular happenstance
and the fate-magma bubbling inside
(i told you i don't believe in fate—you said,
yes,
but i do)

Thump,

Thump, the perpetual freezing /
thump—the virulence, the
white-hot blaze of a heart under the tundra

limestone, basalt heart of memory—
heart of the throughline gone relative at the edges
gone relatively nowhere
except farther than the eye can trace—than the race
can be graced back

longer than the time it takes to hurricane out
the faultlines /

the fissures
in your face
I never watched develop

the fumbling in my verbiage
I never learned to claim

Thump—the residue, the meltwater,
the cascade—archaeological heart—little fossil
record of the memories I can't remember
objectively

the radiance of radio-carbon dating
of the dating of two daring bits of bravery
boldly chasing youth as it dips over the eastern seaboard
the date, I can't remember
the face, I am getting fuzzy (I do not own my vision of you anymore)
the furniture, is all but muddled wood and fragments
but the endless repeating
Thump of the perpetually frozen
fossil
of that heart—those moments—those mummified mirrors
reflecting nothing
rehashing everything

rehearsing nearer and nearer
to only the echo
of a sound;
of a thump
still vibrating
at a volume
I can no longer hear
(and yet I strain)

I kept looking at the horizon

I kept looking at the horizon,
the way the wind
met the courage
of the bones
of the earth

I kept looking for the highway,
the height of something
to transport me
faster than my
patience
would will

I looked across the broken white lines,
I looked across the speeding flash—

You know,
that quantum physics will tell you
the photon
will travel different paths
if it is seen
or unseen

I see this now—the highway river;
the byway sewed together—sequenced yellow and
grids of clouds—I see
the observer observing me /
So I take both paths—the highway going high
and the low-way going tunnelvision;
somewhere beyond what can be measured—
the path which is both paths at once
(until the other collapses—
        crumbling infrastructure, you know?)
That's what quantum physics says,
you know?

I sing ranting lullabies

I sing ranting lullabies
chirping spitfire lunacy—
I sing ranting songs of rolling uphill battles

You pull the hair behind my ear
You wrap your hand in resonance
You curve around my spine

I pull my wallowed legs in
zoos around your thighs

You spin your blood and breath
like anchors round my eyes

I keep singing nonsense rhymes
You whistle tune by tune
I hunger in your ribcage
You open bone by bone

I follow you, you follow back, we traipse into the warmth
I wander down, you wander still, we trace our way back home.

The first time I saw you

The first time I saw you
I saw wrinkled angles and parapets
a tiny home inside your skin
that I might wriggle into

The first time I saw you in a 360-
degree, sweeping shot (camera all the way around
the back of your head)
you were telling me about the sky
you saw once
How the firmament of colors
splayed on the horizon
made you weep
How you had the remnants and ashes
of those colors
tattooed onto your left wrist

The first time I saw your left wrist
held slightly warm against the bonfire
I wept too—those spindly legs
of colors fast faded still saw
what is sometimes apparent—
The glow of invisible strings
wrapped tightly, elegantly, endlessly
from point A to point B

My love—my self—the sea—the torrent—the tattoo
I can still see it
(it's on your skin)

Your head

Your head
like a promise
between my skin
wrapped breathy
and scraggle-hair-scratchy
Your heart like a motion—rippled, tidal
and elegant

Your voice like a resonance—coupled, ancient
and no-longer foreign
and this smell I can never stop smelling

the hunger of your bones for my flesh
the clavicle of my home
where your chest beats
the beat of the drum
hollowing this place
on your breastbone—firm, open,
holding—

All holding, all held

Your head
held—between my hands
or in them

Your head
held—above my heart or within

We talked about a house

We talked about a house, of course
buried underground—something mutinous and romantic
something irresolute in creativity
we talked about a house, of course
and all the lives we'd live

We talked about the fish we'd eat, the way we'd fold our clothes
we talked like empires, we fought like conquerors
we fumbled for the remote
we buried plants like rubbled ashes
we came up spluttering for air

We talked about a house,
sunken low and draped in green—curtailed moss
and dandelion chins

We talked about a river—a time
for rolling in
we talked about the waves
and how to roll back out again

this tiny forgetting

I forgot the street names where i live;
their scattered remembrance hits my brain like
wild arrows splintering

I escaped the cold; the mumbling highways, the riveting
drama of my tiny life, the final tune that the river
makes at day's end
I circled our country in a tiny white cylinder of metal
and i let my brain forget
what the street signs look like
and how the clock chimes incessantly—the day's plans
grabbing me by the neck and sending me down the road;
the endless roads—the rapture of the car's ignition firing
in a panic—in the rush towards some destination
whose name i have cleverly forgotten

The place of my life floods me again
like a memory too ripe to be eaten
I catch the windmill of my heart battering over
every cobbled bridge, every winter-struck
blade of grass
I find my life has been waiting there for me,
that i never quite escaped it—just the atmosphere,
briefly, and the speed limits that catch me by surprise
as i turn endlessly down these roads dotted with
the most mundane of names (the ones i know by heart,
but at this moment have forgotten)

Let me hold this tiny memory loss for a moment
this tiny blank of a mind
waiting to be filled
again
full
to the brim
of chalk lines
waiting to be erased

Great feats accomplished mid-air on a flight home to Philadelphia

You bubble-eye up at me,
faucets of hands pouring out at me
marshmallow skin and brandied hair
swaying without reason in no direction at all

something shouts from inside your tin-pipe of a
crackle-voice—the "Mom!"
escaping into the plane-recycled-air; popping hot
like a cascade of visible letters

I try to pull my sing-song voice out of
the front-most of my quiet-box mouth machine //
you rub your eyes with grandeur,
I press a tiny finger to my lips, make the everlasting "sh" sound

But the air is filled with the tingle of your voice now;
the light through the tiny plane windows reverberates
with the magnet tenor of your high-cathedral-ceilinged voice //
To me it sounds like candy; but still I laugh and "sh" a gentle stream
of fingers pressed against lips and
lilypad eyes glaring a soft "no"

You care only for the joy of sound;
the exuberant declaration:
"Mom! I did it"

(you've done it,
the perfect accomplishment of play;
the greatest accomplishment on the plane)

You bubble-eye your little boy blues at me
I stroke your plum jam cheek;
I secretly thrill myself in the sweet carol of your voice
I cannot stand to quiet your celebratory hum, but here yet again
I press my lips to the tinctures of your ears
for a gentle reminder

(I've done it;
the perfect accomplishment)

and still, after you have quieted
and the anxiety of the passengers on the plane has
released
the jinglelove of your little voice
tingles inside of my brain
like the most elegant
bird still in flight;
a great gift still singing

I follow

I follow the courage of
bare feet across the genealogical map—
Past Kentucky; Broken Arrow;
Names that place themselves at the
back of my tongue; slide down my
throat, but cannot be swallowed /
I consume this history—easy;
words on paper—letters on
carved rocks—headstones
on new grass and depleted soil /
clay rubbed eyelashes—your heart
pearled into the oxygen of the
atmosphere
like so many ancestors
curling towards the sky //
Tiny ridges on the hillside;
roots digging towards the hollow
light of the earth; nothing insignificant;
nothing not worth
reaching towards;
everything somewhere;
or all at once
in its own
place
just where it has always been

I follow the path, the past, the part of the
place misplaced from where it partook in the
participation of
the present

I follow the courage
of so many bare foot steps
(whose prints have long since
blown away in the wind)
but whose clay rubbed wishes
still find me in the

roots
reaching towards the hollow light of the earth;
nothing insignificant; nothing
not worth
reaching towards

All you can measure

Two black holes;
I am, i am
spiraling towards an infinite pool—
of matter, or how it matters, or the mingling of
Time + space

they say {now}
that they'll collide, form one
massive
turnstyle of gravity
pulling in light like a circus tent

they say the waves
will tilt through the atmosphere, sift like
gaseous wishes willing themselves through every
bit of borrowed meaning / will tumble and twist
and contort every shape / will pull through my body
(moving a particle or two)

And the tiniest pieces of my heart
will register
the way it moved through
you, and the tiniest core of my brain
will pulse
one particle at a time
towards spiraling
towards that silent collision
into one

they say everything will matter, everything
leaves traces, everything pulses, everything
sends out meaning; gravitational waves
or the sound of the world chirping back
or the sound of the sun singing light
into day
or the sound of our threads pulling
pulling;

towards;
towards
And finally

(the waves will be all you can measure)

I never wanted to know

I never wanted to know
what missing you would feel like;

But now, (without a doubt)
the cement bounces back
every little memory;
Certainly, the trees' barks are covered
in your laughter
and the buried breaths we drew like shapes
are fossilized in air

the damp ache in my blood /
the old restlessness in my ligaments /
the endless parade of old cliches that
drag themselves to my doorstep /

I patchwork-fantasy my brain back
together—I cobble old smells of tea and burnt
popcorn into my sensory repertoire

I hold these little sieves of
sense memory in my hands—
Something to hold on to;
The taste of saturday afternoons
on your couch;
or the sound of our teeth being
brushed together in unison at 2am

I hold these little whispers of a life
I bundle them; kindling—
Something to light a fire with //
I watch it glow;
ember ash turns fireflies of us all

the sun is setting over the ocean in this poem and i am 35,000 feet in the air

But no one that ever escaped the atmosphere
was ever carrying this much baggage, you say
i—sparkle-toppled from the sky—out the airplane window
dusting coral reef eyes across the ever-
burning horizon

But i, i reply, have never been one
to hold any weight to gravity—and here, the reverse
osmosis of the endless earth stretching out across
the every pink and blue—the mindless hue
that minds not
where i came from
or where we're going;

the fertile ocean pulls nothingsongs
from the drip-drooping sun;
A silent prayer to the graciousness of color

i keep ascending (or the plane does, and i am inside of it,
so it bouys me along, my helpless strings anchored to the ground and all)
whistling to the down-belowers
all the resistance songs to gravity
that tap together in color and hue

The color keeps ascending (or the tilt of the earth keeps turning,
and the color is inside our brains, so it bouys my cells along)

i gape; the color holes me up
holds the perfect landscape of the sea
in my seeing-glass-eye

and gravity does not pull me back down the helpless
choute of strings i am convinced
i am anchored to the ground by

when i gape; too held by color

and the endless configuration of matter,—
i forget that i too, am held by the perfection
of my own weight; that we are all held
by the endless equation of being just enough
for gravity

Which bouys us along;
our helpless strings anchored to the ground and all

And nothing keeps me tied to my own gravity
When i realize i am inside of it
And it bouys me along;
Helpless strings trying to anchor me and the

endless configuration of the density of matter
Which matters only just enough
To prove that we always matter

With mine

I peek my eagle eyes

into your everywhere chest;
the pummel of musculature i hide
my woven bones into

I perch my reticent chin
on the curved momentum of your shoulder blade
Wing-ed; this peace here,
this piece of you that pieces into mine

I craft myself a nest of your hobble hair-ed back,
the intricacies of body and hormone,
a supple delicacy

You cup my head in your hands,
graceful, ever-gentle,
finger-tipped and tooth-grazed;
your smile imprinted in
my imperfections

I tapestry myself towards the
threads of your words, your heart;
a resting place—your voice, a
reverent song, an everywhere
presence, the soothing rapture
of your wilderness entwined
with mine

I; motionless

your ripped
gap-toothed smile
burns into a letter;
flames into the cruelty of
apathy—
the folded hands at the side of the room;
Your narcissism like a potted plant in the corner /
the brashness of your brassy-eyed stare
staring back at me

You toss words like apple-edged daggers—
your careless wind turbine of a larynx

I; motionless, watch as my
throat closes up
like a closet of old air
and stolen explanations

I; my words, my little brain-
rupture; self-defense mechanisms
defending me already—hiding
my voice in the tornado shelter /
with or without willingness,
my voice is an unstringed
instrument

I; silent symphony towards you
with a blank mind, with an empty
rifle, I; scramble-brain
watch you light the room on fire
watch you spin the words; marble-run running
and no rules
on gravity
the marbles will roll whichever ways
they like
in this room

And I; little mute-box stand against
the weight of the storm
dress myself in waiting
and hope my clothes are not flammable /
I press into the gravity of the earth,
hoping the laws of physics still exist,
something solid beneath me
I; paralysis, stand next to my trauma and
wait
for the storm to pass;
for the weight of this wind to blow air
back into my voice

The swollen travellers

the cracked mountainsides—the
fervor of violence peering out of the
landscape—the cliffside; their own caskets—
this country;
does it hold violence innately in its grooves and ridges?
do the firmaments and groping
peaks and valleys
hold the impetus for war within
their sacred structures?
the illness—is it baked into the mantel?
the crust of this country tis of thee
the bareboned lament to the sky

how terribly our destiny manifested itself
upon the crest of these golden hills
how rapturously we throw ourselves into the
oblivion of our own restlessness

how much wilderness is in our body
and how do we tie it down?
how do we sit upon this gracious bundle of earth
and know nothing but the relative comfort of our own feet
upon it

when will we ascend the parapet
and not see it as our own

or are we the swollen travellers misguided
or are we the swollen travellers lost

the daring

your face, light splashed
in the saturn light of the starburst
six flags sound-river;
a twinkle of lights catching your face
out of the light of the moon,
wide-eyed child faced joy,
never-old-for-one-moment joy,

hand brush current of electricity joy;
the safety of your chest where
my secrets are buried, joy—
And the list of wounds
we both inflicted on one another
tucked just out of sight for the time being—

the ocean of starting over;
the pale-light of rushing towards the slow
drip of a lifetime walking towards us
if we dare to meet it;
And our courage—fringed at the edges,
burned at the corners,
enough to rub together to light a spark /
Or just shallow enough to bathe in,
just deep enough to wash ourselves clean?
or just thin enough to never be able to drown

the drip of a lifetime walking towards us
if we dare to meet it

And the sound of the words i keep pursed
between my lips—
the fearful resonance of rejection a
path i dare not walk

the daring bravery of the light, to catch your face
so effortlessly, so silver-gold;
the finest prize i have yet to amount to,

the sound of your heart beating out of key with mine,
And the endless daring of the light—pulling
us ever closer to a lifetime walking
towards us,
if we dare to meet it

I hear your hands

I hear your hands unshackle my
heart from its drawstring purse;
shake out the bees
from my leftover knees and
carry me out into the light again—

here I twist my spine into a straw
to slurp up
the golden air of what you tell
me is a new day

here this little blushing bundle of
nerves pulls itself out of the cataclysm;
brushes itself out of the mossy
overgrown trunks of trees gone by;
ages left dry and pages left scratchless /
here I ratchet towards something
you tell me to trust:
the breeze; or the new sun;
or the way the light is coming
from the sun—you tell me to believe
it's coming from the sun and not from the moon
and I learn to believe
that it is anything less than starlight
filtered through the endless canopy
of green (now yellowed at the edges)
now falling through it
slowly
tenderly
like a wish
like a tenderness I do not deserve

Tin house

Your cupped tenderness
and an old softness to your skin
I have barely allowed myself to remember;
a hollowed shape in your chest
where my head belongs

the firmness of gratitude as it
swells through my body;
the light from my eyelashes
peering through any remnant of you
left on my body /
my skin; the ageless path we flutter down;
two butterflies angling towards one another—
ready to skim the sweetness
off of any cut-flower-hand
ready to scoop it all for our own
tiny legs
to never be dragged down
by weightless love

And my heart like a tin house
clattering in the rain
all sounds heard
all angles visible
all drops pounding a cacophony;
just sonically audible—
and the storm—
not knowing which way to blow:
towards me or away from me;
or inevitably, without care
as to where I wish I wasn't already standing //

and the fertile grass,
the only thing that knows
where the rain should be—
and me, dreaming the storm is about me,
and the tin house, dreaming to be free

of the metaphor once more
—and the soil, the worms, the greedless
seeds tucked in safely—the only things
that know what the rain is for—
and me, the endless story wafter—believing
this storm is my pain made visible
—and the invisible: just
raining
its own secret
tremendous rain

skeleton

radioactive love,
this mountain of moving music //
the miles from my eyes to yours;
the stretched distance which
becomes thin upon listening /
the curvature of sound which
never makes it from my lips to yours /
the desperation of angled skin cells;
hunting for one another;
like a desolate skeleton of
love once-discarded;
always buried;
never burned;
ashen in cruelty;
and firmly, fearlessly;
still alive

On the carousel with my son, aged 5

I will not trade this
moment for anything, thank you—
not the patterned lullaby etched
around your neck;
nor the fruit-budded lilypie of
the carousel tumbling by;
Your blue and white striped
zebra-horse bobbing up and down;
the twinklebugs of mid-day
dancing round the perfect sound
of this little 3-minute ride;
your half-sized hand
plunged into mine; fearlessly
firmly; freely

I would not trade the moments
with you that have cobbled us
together like monuments /
I have cherished the silent color-flash
of your hot pink cape trusted around
your shoulders—you brave boy in a bold world
I have cherished the everyhum, the
giggledrum, the mutant and
half-sung melody that
melts us together like madness

I will keep holding your tiny hand
in mine, as long as this carousel keeps
twirling us; magic-footed and astride a
purple-maned monster horse; i will
keep holding your hand so you will not
fall—the endless ornaments of light
dotting the constellations of passing electricity //
the brief, bumbling ride that spins in circles—
over faster than you can laugh //
ready to ride again
to learn how to sit taller on the back of this

bucking wild thing
all by yourself
your half-sized hand
plunged into mine; fearlessly
firmly; freely

Crimson, orange + lemon yellow

radiant day + lamplight afternoon, the silent wishes of a thousand leaves playing in harmony with the light—the gentle wish of autumn, to carry itself through every bending branch—to transform the formed, to resonate inside the cellular singular singing voices of the grass, the grain, the hurried rain—the fumbled moments that sit outside of your brain—the lenses that tap at the glass of your eyes, that ask to come in, that do not bring anything with them but air and gold—the streaks of summer sliding out of the spines of green—the cascading hues all across the landscape—circumnavigating the residual blues and violets and sinking in to all that crimson, orange + lemon yellow—yellow as far as the eye can see, the splendor of falling in to color over and over again, the palette of your heart just a beating thing, a fearless wing of a season turning over and over—reclaiming the word change, reclaiming the world that continues to change, whether we fall with it or not

The slow saving

And here a gash,
a small pinprick of pickled prickly-ings
of feelings, reelings, curled buttons on cobbled coats,
turncoat tapestries of time, and here;

And here, a lash—
The first blood-letting of you letting me
go, letting me flow
over the edge like a gaseous substance;
like a viscous ooze gooping away;
slow moving, slow go-letting
and still stuck to the surface i am /
trying to escape (the nature of goop, you know)

And here, a crash;
the smash-bundle peel of a
trainwreck in half-motion /
Everything slow, everything
pummeling the side of gravity
with a flaccid pick

No one wants to change it, no one
knows how to
want to know
how to stop it

So we let it slow-ooze in reverse
the muddle mash of a mess of moments
striking in solid silence /

Here a gash;
bandaged before the bloodflood
But still oozing, molten—viscous;
vicious

The singular

the singular hue mixed;
burnished crimson + aquamarine
I put my hands inside of the
face of the future
I let them fumble ageless-ly with the door key

I let my fossilized bones name myself;
Tyrannosaur; tyrant; troublesome
I carve my back into an arch violent
enough the spark a fire

I let the chill thrill through the air
for just a minute longer
before I let the boundless
grace of spring sing through the rivers
of the sky
I trace myself towards the
everlasting outline of the new gods
The firm Herculean rapture of something
waiting to be born

I heart aquaphor smart discover
Rattle-bones
only the new season / only the daffodil scent
Of the new day / only a field of wide-eyed endlessness
looking towards the horizon
once again a passport of crouched dandelion
whispering a song of plated hieroglyphs
no one can teach you

when you look and you see the
reflection of the grass staring back at you

 no one but anyone will be reborn again
the way that this Earth will be reborn again
and everyone always will follow

Of course,

Of course, she says,
of course,
no other way could this possibly have ended
no other way could my heart feel the bitter taste of regret so violently

other than you dropping the phone at the end of the line,
an endless plastic line of webbing drawing all of the fools to the table

You didn't do anything wrong,
you say; I say

I capsized first
you, drawing the end of the life raft towards you like a blanket—
I always knew I say;
your words tip like the finality
of a star feeding itself with its own fire—
(the metaphors are strong here, the words are weak;
the magnetic force is quantum; neverending and pink)

Of course my heart would butter-churn and evaporate
at the sound of your footsteps walking away—
how could I never not always know that?
Of course my mind would splinter cell and cut all the corners;
how could that not be laced into my DNA?

And this trauma too—
will it too be laced into my DNA?
Passed down the endless line?
When do the chromosomes bend back in,
armor up and fold over in rebellion //
new patterns and arrangements, the strongest fight there is; when does it
wash out?

Now submerging

You gallup-giggle, splash through the suds,
a lump of fresh soap bubbles, the finest joy
this side of the Delaware river;
something profane transcended
in the plastic blue body of your flying dolphin,
soaring through this afternoon's ocean—
our own barrier reef in the bathroom—
leaping, this dolphin
as he flies towards patchwork tan tile—
the wildest adventure in the neighborhood—
screech shout and slosh about;
now mush muddle and flop about;
now Donnie the dolphin floats
effortlessly towards the triumph of the steel spout,
sugar spice and everything meaningful—
now swirling, now submerging, now surfacing—
the sight; the singing sounds
of so much
important work being done

I hollow towards the light

i, rabbit horn, sea monster, rattle death—i call sadness into my ribcage to light fire to my heart. i mourn the afternoons bathed in autumn light through the rose curtains. i mourn the ring of singing voices in hollowed tree stumps. i fear the bones of winter crackling towards the sky without relent. i fear the branches; the harness of the sky to the earth. i fear myself. i search myself. i become more of myself. i hark to the light. to the purpose that petals my feet forward. i hollow towards the light. i hear my own whispers; i repeat action and action and action and i rest not wearily enough. i hunger, i rattle, i raise. i reach towards the light—i keep reaching.

When

When the afternoon sun peeled away at the tiny
cells of our brave skin—when we jumped off the high rocks
30 feet in the air
and my heart heat fluttered after yours, the gum trees
splattered like muted symphonies;
the ancient call of wild birds slicing through the window
the morning question tapping at my cupboard
Weetabix and the change in my tongue
that changed for you
the endless cacophony of waves that rolled towards us
a snake peeking out of the bush,
the air filled with starlight; the southern cross
streaming over our heads like a pile of prayers
to the modern world—
to find the thread at the bottom of the rainbow serpent
and follow it like a kite
letting the wind blow you
and your feet walk you
towards horizons made more magical
with every blink you break

We tied our love inside a bottle, tossed
it down the river, let the goop of the ages
mix with algae, seaweed and all our wishes for the future
—it caught fire, it was swallowed by pollution,
it was buffeted by a hurricane;
and still it bobs,
a little map home
whenever the Dreaming calls me
again

the thursday after last tuesday three years ago

When did our love die?
as the silent fumbling fingers for the door key
gazed staringly at the spider curling its
way across the windshield?

As I hurled my heart across the room
like a frisbee, projectile bouncing against every
soft reminder of the things we never owned?

Or was it when I placed the orange in
the palm of your hand
gingerly, but not gingerly enough
tenderly, but somehow too tenderly

Or was it the day the sun arrived inside our house
burning through the filament in the lightbulbs
twisting through the lampshades
and capsizing the curtains

Was it after the spider-bite? When I
rolled in ashes on the bed, when my skin fell off
and the hospital said at least I wasn't dead

Perhaps it was the thursday after last tuesday three years ago
when all at once and all at last
with no particular hurricane;
the wind blew through this room
and carried you away

We three kings

We three kings
piled high with ring-sings
of the roller-derby of our
Years, piled next to one another
in concentric circles
circling the sky,
Piling low onto the rooted fumble
of the wish
of our reflection
to meet
half past the radiation
of the shadow cast
by the aged sun age-ing
us against the earth

We three captives of chlorophyll
captains of this corner of the world
coronation of the curdled seeds
of tomorrow never blossoming

We three carriers of story bones,
of storm homes,
of wander eyes wandering without lies
with the geyser of growing
glimpsing the gargantuan
chasm we endlessly
root towards;
The wild chasm
we endlessly
grow up out of;
Scrambling towards the light /
or towards the storm /
Or towards the story
half-told mid-flight
where we remain
always king of shadows never cast

Prayer for my son, aged 5

this candle you hold in the
waxy residue between
me and you
Still holds light

this rampart of the day folding
at the crease on the horizon;
the purple hue of sunlight
dripping through the strands
of your hair

this light—no light brighter
than your tiny hands,
your bubble-guppy eyes
gulping the sunrise like medicine

this little wish we make together;
that our hands will always fit inside one another's,
that your body,
when it grows out of fitting inside my lap
will race the sun as fast as the wind
will let you /
And that you will let me
stand in the billow
of the breeze you will blow;
watch as the rays filter out of your hands
to make what only
you can make

No horizon on the map

Ah—no horizon on the map

Only lines, figures, demarcations
destinations, reverberations, time-lapsed imitations
radioactive limitations, miles-full of instigations and instant-nations.

And stories /
or a hand,
at least,
Reaching
towards

an ocean (an opening)

Quarantine, day 51

the days sing quietly now
the silent song of
May breeze and the lilting
necks of trees gone
buckling at the sides

The days roll wide and aimless
but fervent with the
gift of clocks gone dry /

I race my fingers to the edge
of the wall and back again
to imagine once more
the weight of anything
needing to be done

But what i feel instead
is the perfect press of skin
on plastered paint;
the resonance of cells on
something hard and firm

The respite here; on this beige wall
lies within the structure;
the radical ability to maintain
as all other particles seem to dip
and sway with quantum indifference

The wall sings quietly,
you are still here
you are still here
And when the world tips insideout
i will be here too

When I was a one-celled prokaryote

When i was a one-celled prokaryote;
when i learned to stretch myself into two;
when i pulled myself towards a nucleus
when understanding dawned like a pair
of fresh hands reaching—
i played records on my circular body,
i swam into the sunset and called it
nothing at all
i mounded myself in piles and could not
think of why—

or perhaps the thoughts
were so thick—so molasses wild
and honey cream—that i became the thoughts
themselves, a consciousness
coronating itself on the side of a volcano /
a singularly held cell of everythingthought
thinking into existence
the need for mops and windex;
the urge for half-cracked windows
and neatly folded newspapers
i thought these things into the sea
and the sea floated me the shore
the half-baked promise of always more

Strung together

You leap into the new day;
four fingers stretched towards the sun—rapturous in
the bounce on the bed
the ever-reaching; the pummeling of feet into my ribcage;
the curled 'i love you' into the side of my skull with a
fistful of hair and a pocket full of loose string and
found pebbles

you, google-hair and giggle-eyed; you press
some secret joke between yourself and the
jiggles of my belly
gasping for laughter
(the punchline escapes me, but the
sound of your laughter does not)

You / inexhaustible song-box do not whine at the sun
but gallop towards it with a fervor
that nearly sets my pillow ablaze
(and almost nearly the lamp too, as you tug effortlessly on its cord)

I hear you hum to yourself—the tiniest remembering
of the gentlest heart—the words strung together with a thick cord
(words still rubbing one another with newness and grandeur
when placed next to one another)

I hum to myself as well—the tiniest remembering;
the most graceful gift of 'i love you'—the words
strung together with a thick cord

The rally cry

the rally cry strikes the sky;
Sharp—pierces the cloud grumble;
we hunt and hunger across the pavements
of all our city streets
in our town squares
on our lowly sidewalks
we call justice with a fervor
we call out the blood-stained hands as we see them
—quick—Sharp
We do not forget a name
We call our fists into the air
more than a prayer
louder than a wish
fiercer than a knife; our fists
the great harkening towards the open sky we all deserve
towards the air we all deserve to breathe
We walk through the ancestral lines carved for us
We listen to the pain we cannot claim as our own
we ask for our own hands to reach
towards the knowledge we have ignored //
we do not beg for a better world, we demand it /
loudly, with no apology,
and no relenting—
we carve it ourselves,
with the ages and ages of injustices
spurning us on, filling our hands
with the knowledge to know what to do,
to know how to ask those that do,
to know how to humble ourselves
towards the only fight worth fighting for

Superposition

superposition of, everything at the same time
Or/ the sine wave
of several signs
pointing towards
ten trillion words
you already know how to say
inside your ribcage
but cannot translate
into blood or matter

the quantum courage
Of everything at the same time
to remain somehow what they are
to not flip,
dip through this side of
the universe to the other side—
to one, somehow,
more true,
astounds my somehow
still stable cells—
      And which, that astoundment
        in and of itself—is a greater
          majesty than any black hole

the cell's awareness of awareness;
what a constant
barrage of oceanic wonder
sits inside of my silly lump of
brain cells
waiting for you
to break through the barrier of cells with me
and come swim
in the superposition
of everything all at the same time

Only

Roll out the reticence to move
towards any direction
except right here—right to the Right,
to the never-ending quest at being right;
the Left left with only the leftovers of
leaving the people out of the people's party;
The general effort towards siphoning
the general election
into a visual feast of
fastidious forrays
into moral fasting
—waiting until the
—waiting until
the right Right moment
to push towards the left
Just enough to push offshore
to row a little farther
into the deep Blue sea
of seeing what is only available
when we all see it at the same time;
When the people's presence
pushes towards the present—
a slide across the sleight of hand;
a surface tension tightening
its grip on the curtain
of theatrics about to be pulled back;
Not Left or Right,
but endlessly back
into the past we all passed through
to get to the never progressing future
of never forward-ism
of sliding the wheel sideways and neither direction at all—
Just away
from that moral arc of the universe
ever pointing towards
just
us

Between

The way you kiss me goodnight;
gentle; a soft wish
on the top of my forehead
fingers interlaced like a web;
wide-eyed fireflies calling for me
through your veins:

the way your tender heart cups
mine like a prayer
like a secret between the August sky
and me—
The porch light glowing; the green grass
swaying in the darkness
Honey-blossom alive with the
secret song between our lips;
between my heart and yours
trapped and tumbled in the little
space of air
between

Historic courthouse, centreville, maryland

Hollowed out firmament of Justice;
bricks painted white,
stacked by hands whose ash now
billows about the roots of these structures:
these structures that never deteriorate,

the perfect path lined with green grass,
the perfect lilies placed around a statue of Queen Anne;
the endless monarchy and oligarchy of
something we come to pray to:
the precipice of judgement whose
hand sits in gavels long-since hammered away;
hammering away sentences, not paragraphs—
just sound bites, not full context—
just pieces of pieces of lives lost;
and laws held and upheld like a handful
of marbles jangling,
with all the light that passes through them,
and all the air that sits at the
edge of the spherical shape;

the way we hold on to history
like a sack full of old coins that no longer hold any value—
but the sound of the jangle
pleases our ear so;
the jangle of the jail cells ring too;
the clink of old metal and salvaged
chunks of wrought iron that once
brought the iron fist to some wishless land;
the wishlist landed on this lapping shoreland;
this Plymouth Rock-edged cliff;
the sound of the jangle observes us observing it;
and continues to sing

By now

By now I'm sure your hands
have moved into another dimension;
holding a child of yours
whose mother is not me
By now I'm sure your heart has
formed great walls against me—
thick ice-shackled, and sharp-edged
I'm sure you have burned all the letters
we etched into cyberspace
the thousand I love yous
that race around in the internet—
The never erasable pixels
a representation
of something that could only be
laced between two pairs
of eyes on a shoreline in endless youth

By now I'm sure the crackle sound
of my name holds no sting
but just sits flat in the air
like a ghost that cannot haunt,
Casper, or something even friendlier

By now I'm sure you can't even remember
the time we laughed ourselves
all the way home, the night you sat
with me on the sidewalk outside the bar
when I had to lay down on the
cement just to stop the stars from spinning,

By now I'm sure the tides have all
come in; I'm sure the tabs have all been
paid; the sketched blueprint of our house
on the hill has become a real house now,
with someone else laying next
to you each night, placing the glass
of water on the bedside, stroking your
hair as it lay on the pillow

The thought of your baby's
cupped head lying on your chest
has me swollen, heaving up on to shore,
in stitches, floating out to outer space,
waiting to form the exoskeleton of a new planet,
waiting for ten supernova to renew my skin,
restart at the bottom of a black hole,
reach towards new light, form a new star,
a thousand red dwarfs shaded the color of your eyes

Upwards towards my skin

slinklove, you pile your hands upwards towards my skin—a bottle-nosed dolphin and something mammalian and curved—like the willow of a spine, the petercottontail of a clavicle. bones; rapturous, rattling against one another—flesh: hollow, formed, willing, perpetual. windowpane of your eyes/ they keep approaching, following, leveling. is it your shape or your circumstance i find myself in? is it this bed or this hurricane i keep myself bonded to? is it proximity? this thing—desire—is it close to me? or the closeness to the sea (which heralds me back, and in heralding, bonds me—keeps me never approaching anything other than the brine of the sea)

is it intimacy, or the sea calling me back? is it ever approaching? your skin/ the nape of your circumstance / my hunger / lust, or something language approaches; like teeth

is it skin; a shell; a sea
or the shore, lapping back?

Semi-permafrost

The redwoods awake; unscathed,
laughing at us—some ancient
gossip passes
through the roots, back to the
superbugs asleep in the permafrost
We wait, ripping ourselves apart—pulling
ourselves to bits while the trunks
of trees that have stretched wide for
Millenia
sing their own laughter songs
to one another: reckless species
reckless sons and daughters
that have let the Amazon burn;
that have let Australia burn
that have let the poles slink back;
tucking their white socks in to their shoes

Still prepossessed
with the self-obsessed
with the richness of time and space
that bends and contours around the
liminal trace of our skin—the shape of
our bones reaching out of our cheeks

The way our skulls will look
as they swelter in the coming heat;
the way they will
Peel away from our foundation,
our blush, as the mascara
squeals its way off our lashes
and the heat pulls out the ancient
stories once buried in ice—now carried
on the wind

The permafrost, now only semi-permafrost
and us, only semi-permanent as well

And the redwoods still laugh,
careen towards the endless wisdom
of being rooted deeper than the wind can shake

Lauren Suchenski has a difficult relationship with punctuation and loves to watch the leaves change color. She has been nominated twice for the Pushcart Prize and four times for The Best of the Net. She is also the author of two chapbooks: *Full of Ears and Eyes Am I* (Finishing Line Press) and *All Atmosphere* (Selcouth Station). You can find more of her writing on Instagram @lauren_suchenski or on Twitter @laurensuchenski. Most of all, she enjoys collecting rocks and staring at the stars with her son.

www.ingramcontent.com/pod-product-compliance
Lightning Source LLC
Chambersburg PA
CBHW021202090426
42740CB00008B/1197